griddling

p

This is a Parragon Book
First published in 2004

Parragon
Queen Street House
4 Queen Street
Bath BA1 1HE, UK

HB ISBN: 1-40543-715-4
PB ISBN: 1-40543-719-7

Printed in China

Produced by the Bridgewater Book Company Ltd.
Project Designer: Michael Whitehead
Project Editor: Anna Samuels
Home Economists: Sara Hasketh, Richard Green

Note for the Reader
This book uses metric and imperial measurements. Follow the
same units of measurement throughout; do not mix metric and
imperial. All spoon measurements are level: teaspoons are
assumed to be 5 ml and tablespoons are assumed to be 15 ml.
Unless otherwise stated, milk is assumed to be full fat, eggs and
individual vegetables such as potatoes are medium, and pepper
is freshly ground black pepper. .

Recipes using raw or very lightly cooked eggs should be avoided
by infants, the elderly, pregnant women, convalescents, and
anyone suffering from an illness.

contents

introduction

GRIDDLING is a very easy and quick method of cooking that nowadays is becoming more and more popular. This way of cooking is seen also as a healthy method of cooking. The recipes are easy and are ideal for entertaining or for a quick snack. They can be served during the day or for evening events.

While grilling is carried out over an open heat, griddling takes place on a closed, solid surface. A griddle is a special flat pan, with a ridged base, that is designed to cook food with a minimum of fat or oil. A griddling pan is usually made of a thick, heavy metal that is a good heat conductor and some pans have a non-stick coating. They usually have long handles, like a frying pan, or some have handgrips on opposite sides. A griddle is the key equipment that you will need, but skewers, wooden sticks, cocktail sticks or toothpicks are also necessary for some of the recipes. These items need to be prepared beforehand. Check that the skewers will fit your particular make of griddle as those that have handles may not. If you are using wooden sticks, you need to soak them in water first for about half an hour to prevent them from burning. Cocktail sticks or toothpicks make very good skewers for griddled canapés as do sprigs of rosemary or lemon grass.

Please be aware that, because this particular method of cooking leads to the griddling pan becoming very hot, you may have to open the windows in your kitchen.

The art of griddling is a way of cooking that concentrates on the flavours of one or two key ingredients. Sauces in griddling need to be prepared separately rather than being cooked with the main ingredients and the main focus is in the use of marinades and contrasting dressings.

In the meat section, a variety of marinades are presented. All marinades need to be covered carefully with clingfilm and left to refrigerate for the number of hours specified in each recipe. The

lamb chops in the Minted Lamb Chops recipe, for example, need to be left in the refrigerator for two hours and turned during this period so that the meat absorbs the flavours of the yogurt, garlic, ginger, coriander seeds and salt and pepper. Griddling also offers the opportunity for the creation of tasty kebabs. If you like steaks, and especially hot, spicy steaks, try the Ginger Beef with Chilli recipe. The steaks are left to marinate in a tasty ginger, garlic and ground chilli marinade and then served with a hot chilli relish.

For some exciting griddled poultry dishes, try the Thai Chicken recipe. The marinade is delicious, consisting of lemon grass, garlic, spring onions, ginger, coriander roots, sugar, coconut milk and fish and soy sauce. The Hot Red Chicken recipe is equally tasty but, beware, quite hot! For something

more exotic try the Jamaican Kebabs, the mangoes really bringing a unique flavour to the dish.

Fish and seafood recipes are very varied as there are so many types of fish and seafood. Included are dishes with particularly tasty sauces. The Mexican Tuna recipe is excellent for those who like to eat hot and spicy food as the tuna is served with a particularly hot sauce.

Vegetables are extremely tasty when griddled and can be served as starters or as main course accompaniments. The Aubergines with Tsatziki dish, for example, is ideal as a starter.

Griddled fruit is particularly delicious. Included in the final section of the book is a superb selection of mouthwatering dessert recipes which can be served at the end of a meal or on their own.

meat

GRIDDLING meat is not far off from actually barbecuing meat; meat that has been griddled has a characteristic charcoal appearance and smoky flavour. Included are ten truly quick and easy recipes that draw on a wide variety of meats and offer a range of sauces, marinades and accompaniments.

variation

If you like, substitute the same amount of
fresh parsley for the watercress.

tabasco steaks
with watercress butter

A variation on a classic theme, this simple but rather extravagant dish
would be ideal for a special occasion. *SERVES 4*

1 bunch of watercress
85 g/3 oz unsalted butter, softened
4 sirloin steaks, about 225 g/8 oz each
4 tsp Tabasco sauce
salt and pepper

Using a sharp knife, finely chop enough watercress to fill 4 tablespoons. Reserve a few watercress leaves for the garnish. Place the butter in a small bowl and beat in the chopped watercress with a fork until fully incorporated. Cover with clingfilm and leave to chill in the refrigerator until required.

Sprinkle each steak with 1 teaspoon of the Tabasco sauce, rubbing it in well. Season to taste with salt and pepper.

Preheat the griddle. Cook the steaks over a high heat, 2^1/$_2$ minutes each side for rare, 4 minutes each side for medium and 6 minutes each side for well done. Transfer the steaks to serving plates, garnish with the reserved watercress leaves and serve immediately, topped with the watercress butter.

ginger beef with chilli

Serve these fruity, hot, spicy steaks with noodles. Use a non-stick,
ridged griddle pan to cook with a minimum of fat. *SERVES 4*

4 lean beef steaks, such as rump, sirloin
or fillet, 100 g/3½ oz each
salt and pepper
1 tsp vegetable oil
strips of fresh red chilli, to garnish

marinade

2 tbsp ginger wine
2.5-cm/1-inch piece of
fresh root ginger, finely chopped
1 garlic clove, crushed
1 tsp ground chilli

relish

225 g/8 oz fresh pineapple
1 small red pepper
1 fresh red chilli
2 tbsp light soy sauce
1 piece of stem ginger in syrup, drained
and chopped

Trim any excess fat from the steaks if necessary.
Using a meat mallet or covered rolling pin, pound
the steaks until they are 1 cm/½ inch thick. Season
on both sides with salt and pepper to taste and
place in a shallow dish.

To make the marinade, combine the ginger
wine, fresh root ginger, garlic and ground chilli,
then pour it over the meat. Cover with clingfilm
and chill for 30 minutes.

Meanwhile, make the relish. Peel and finely
chop the pineapple and place it in a bowl. Halve,
deseed and finely chop the red pepper and chilli.
Stir into the pineapple with the soy sauce and stem
ginger. Cover with clingfilm and chill until required.

Brush a ridged griddle pan with the oil and
heat until very hot. Drain the beef and add to the
pan, pressing down to seal. Lower the heat and
cook for 5 minutes. Turn the steaks over and cook
for another 5 minutes.

Drain the steaks on kitchen paper and
transfer to warmed serving plates. Garnish with
chilli strips and serve with noodles, spring onions
and the relish.

to serve
freshly cooked noodles
2 spring onions, shredded

best-ever burgers

These succulent, home-made burgers bear no resemblance to the little ready-made patties available in most shops. *SERVES 6*

900 g/2 lb lean minced steak

2 onions, finely chopped

25 g/1 oz fresh white breadcrumbs

1 egg, lightly beaten

1¹/₂ teaspoons finely chopped fresh thyme

salt and pepper

to serve

6 sesame seed baps

2 tomatoes

1 onion

lettuce leaves

mayonnaise

mustard

tomato ketchup

Place the steak, onions, breadcrumbs, egg and thyme in a large glass bowl and season to taste with salt and pepper. Mix thoroughly using your hands.

Form the mixture into 6 large patties with your hands and a round-bladed knife.

Heat the griddle and cook the burgers on the griddle for 3–4 minutes on each side. Meanwhile, cut the baps in half and briefly toast them. Using a sharp knife, slice the tomatoes and cut the onion into thinly sliced rings. Fill the toasted baps with the cooked burgers, lettuce, sliced tomatoes and onion rings and serve immediately, with the mayonnaise, mustard and tomato ketchup.

variation

For Tex-Mex burgers, add 2 deseeded and
finely chopped fresh green chillies to the
mixture at the same time as the onions
and serve with guacamole.

spicy lamb steaks

Lamb, fresh rosemary and bay leaves always go so well together, and in this delicious dish a hot
and spicy marinade is used to give the lamb an extra-special flavour. *SERVES 4*

4 lamb steaks, about 175 g/6 oz each
8 fresh rosemary sprigs
8 fresh bay leaves
2 tbsp olive oil

spicy marinade
2 tbsp sunflower oil
1 large onion, finely chopped
2 garlic cloves, finely chopped
2 tbsp jerk seasoning
1 tbsp curry paste
1 tsp grated fresh root ginger
400 g/14 oz canned chopped tomatoes
4 tbsp Worcestershire sauce
3 tbsp light muscovado sugar
salt and pepper

To make the marinade, heat the oil in a heavy-based saucepan. Add the onion and garlic and cook, stirring occasionally, for 5 minutes, or until softened. Stir in the jerk seasoning, curry paste and grated ginger and cook, stirring constantly, for 2 minutes. Add the tomatoes, Worcestershire sauce and sugar, then season to taste with salt and pepper. Bring to the boil, stirring constantly, then reduce the heat and simmer for 15 minutes, or until thickened. Remove from the heat and leave to cool.

Place the lamb steaks between 2 sheets of clingfilm and beat with the side of a rolling pin to flatten. Transfer the steaks to a large, shallow, non-metallic dish. Pour the marinade over them, turning to coat. Cover with clingfilm and leave to marinate in the refrigerator for 3 hours.

Drain the lamb, reserving the marinade. Heat the griddle and cook the lamb over a medium–high heat for 5–7 minutes on each side. Meanwhile, dip the rosemary and bay leaves in the olive oil and cook on the griddle for 3–5 minutes. Serve the lamb immediately with the herbs.

minted lamb chops

You can prepare this dish with any kind of lamb chops – leg chops are especially tender – or cutlets, in which case you will probably require two per serving. Shoulder steaks also work well. *SERVES 6*

6 chump chops, about 175 g/6 oz each

150 ml/5 fl oz natural Greek yogurt

2 garlic cloves, finely chopped

1 tsp grated fresh root ginger

1/4 tsp coriander seeds, crushed

salt and pepper

1 tbsp olive oil, plus extra for brushing

1 tbsp orange juice

1 tsp walnut oil

2 tbsp chopped fresh mint

Place the chops in a large, shallow, non-metallic bowl. Mix half the yogurt, the garlic, ginger and coriander seeds together in a jug and season to taste with salt and pepper. Spoon the mixture over the chops, turning to coat, and then cover with clingfilm and leave to marinate in the refrigerator for 2 hours, turning occasionally.

Place the remaining yogurt, the olive oil, orange juice, walnut oil and mint in a small bowl and, using a hand-held whisk, whisk until thoroughly blended. Season to taste with salt and pepper. Cover the minted yogurt with clingfilm and leave to chill in the refrigerator until ready to serve.

Drain the chops, scraping off the marinade. Brush with olive oil and cook on the griddle for 5–7 minutes on each side. Serve immediately with the minted yogurt.

variation

If you like, omit the orange juice and walnut oil and stir in ¹/₄ teaspoon ground star anise and a pinch each of ground cinnamon and ground cumin.

cook's tip

Both red and white onions have a sweeter, milder flavour than brown onions. Spanish onions are also mild, but as they are large, use only 1 and cut it into quarters.

gin & juniper pork

This dish was originally cooked with wild boar, which is now being farmed and is available in some major supermarkets. It is equally delicious when made with pork chops.

SERVES 4

4 pork chops, about 175 g/6 oz each

50 ml/2 fl oz dry gin

175 ml/6 fl oz orange juice

2 red or white onions, cut in half

6 juniper berries, lightly crushed

thinly pared rind of 1 orange

1 cinnamon stick

1 bay leaf

2 tsp finely chopped fresh thyme

salt and pepper

Place the pork chops in a shallow, non-metallic dish. Pour in the gin and orange juice and add the onion halves. Add the juniper berries, orange rind, cinnamon stick, bay leaf and thyme and, using a fork, stir well until the pork chops are thoroughly coated. Cover with clingfilm and leave to marinate in the refrigerator for up to 8 hours.

Drain the pork chops and onions, reserving the marinade. Season the pork chops to taste with salt and pepper and sieve the marinade into a small jug.

Cook the pork and onions on the griddle, brushing frequently with the reserved marinade, for 7–9 minutes on each side, or until thoroughly cooked. Transfer to a large serving plate and serve immediately.

cook's tip

Turkey breast steaks would also be very tasty cooked in this way, but should be griddled for 7–8 minutes on each side. Make sure they are thoroughly cooked before serving.

lemon & herb pork escalopes

Although it is always important that pork is well done, be careful not to overcook these delicately flavoured, thin escalopes and be sure to griddle them only over a medium heat.

SERVES 4

4 pork escalopes
2 tbsp sunflower oil
6 bay leaves, torn into pieces
grated rind and juice of 2 lemons
125 ml/4 fl oz beer
1 tbsp clear honey
6 juniper berries, lightly crushed
salt and pepper
1 crisp dessert apple
fresh flat-leaved parsley sprigs,
to garnish

Place the pork escalopes in a shallow, non-metallic dish. Heat the oil in a small, heavy-based saucepan. Add the bay leaves and stir-fry for 1 minute. Stir in the lemon rind and juice, beer, honey and juniper berries and season to taste with salt and pepper.

Pour the mixture over the pork, turning to coat. Cover with clingfilm, leave to cool, then leave to marinate in the refrigerator for up to 8 hours.

Drain the pork, reserving the marinade. Core the apple and cut into rings. Cook the pork on the griddle, brushing frequently with the reserved marinade, for 5 minutes on each side, or until thoroughly cooked. Cook the apples on the griddle, brushing frequently with the marinade, for 3 minutes. Transfer the pork to a large serving plate with the apple rings, garnish with parsley sprigs and serve immediately.

normandy brochettes

The orchards of Normandy are famous throughout France, providing both eating apples and cider-making varieties. For an authentic touch, enjoy a glass of Calvados between courses. *SERVES 4*

450 g/1 lb pork fillet
300 ml/10 fl oz dry cider
1 tbsp finely chopped fresh sage
6 black peppercorns, crushed
2 crisp eating apples
1 tbsp sunflower oil

Using a sharp knife, cut the pork into 2.5-cm/1-inch cubes, then place in a large, shallow, non-metallic dish. Mix the cider, sage and peppercorns together in a jug, pour the mixture over the pork and turn until thoroughly coated. Cover with clingfilm and leave to marinate in the refrigerator for 1–2 hours.

Drain the pork, reserving the marinade. Core the apples, but do not peel, then cut into wedges. Dip the apple wedges into the reserved marinade and thread onto several metal skewers, alternating with the cubes of pork. Stir the sunflower oil into the remaining marinade.

Cook the brochettes on the griddle over a medium heat, turning and brushing frequently with the reserved marinade, for 12–15 minutes. Finally, transfer the brochettes to a large serving plate and, if you prefer, remove the meat and apples from the skewers before serving. Serve immediately.

variation

Replace 1 apple with 6 no-soak dried prunes
wrapped in strips of streaky bacon. Thread
the prunes onto the skewers with the
remaining apple and pork.

cook's tip
It is worth taking the time to find a
good-quality soy sauce for the aromatic
marinade that flavours these chops. Chinese
supermarkets stock the best range of sauces.

soy pork with coriander

The spicy, Eastern-style flavours that suffuse these pork chops will make them an unusual and original favourite. *SERVES 4*

Place the pork chops in a large, shallow, non-metallic dish. Crush the coriander seeds and peppercorns in a spice mill. Alternatively, place in a mortar and crush with a pestle. Place the soy sauce, garlic, sugar, crushed coriander seeds and peppercorns in a jug and stir well until the sugar has dissolved.

Pour the soy sauce mixture over the chops, turning to coat. Cover with clingfilm and then leave to marinate in the refrigerator for 1 hour, turning occasionally.

Drain the chops, reserving the marinade, and then cook them on the griddle over a medium–high heat, brushing frequently with the reserved marinade, for 7–10 minutes on each side. Transfer to a large serving plate, garnish with fresh coriander sprigs and serve.

4 pork chops, about 175 g/6 oz each

1 tbsp coriander seeds

6 black peppercorns

4 tbsp dark soy sauce

1 garlic clove, finely chopped

1 tsp sugar

fresh coriander sprigs, to garnish

griddled pork
with orange sauce

In this recipe, the pork is garnished with gremolata, a popular Italian seasoning mixture with a citrus tang, which gives the dish a refreshing summery flavour. *SERVES 4*

4 tbsp freshly squeezed orange juice

4 tbsp red wine vinegar

2 garlic cloves, finely chopped

pepper

4 pork steaks, trimmed of all visible fat

olive oil, for brushing

gremolata

3 tbsp finely chopped fresh parsley

grated rind of 1 lime

grated rind of ¹/₂ lemon

1 garlic clove, very finely chopped

Mix the orange juice, vinegar and garlic together in a shallow, non-metallic dish and season to taste with pepper. Add the pork, turning to coat. Cover and leave in the refrigerator to marinate for up to 3 hours.

Meanwhile, mix all the gremolata ingredients in a small mixing bowl, cover with clingfilm and leave to chill in the refrigerator until required.

Heat a griddle pan and brush lightly with olive oil. Remove the pork from the marinade, reserving

the marinade, add to the pan and cook over a medium–high heat for 5 minutes on each side, or until the juices run clear when the meat is pierced with a skewer.

Meanwhile, pour the marinade into a small saucepan and simmer over a medium heat for 5 minutes, or until slightly thickened.

Transfer the pork to a serving dish, pour the orange sauce over it and sprinkle with the gremolata. Serve immediately.

variation

This dish would work equally well with chicken breast portions. Remove the skin from the cooked chicken before serving.

poultry

FOR those with a penchant for chicken, turkey or duck, try one of these griddled poultry recipes. Included are spicy, hot and milder recipes that draw on a range of herbs.

thai chicken

Roadside stalls serve meals and snacks throughout the day and night in every Thai city. Spicy chicken is the number one favourite. This spicy chicken recipe is delicious served with a green salad.

SERVES 4

Place the chicken in a single layer in a large, shallow, non-metallic dish. Put the lemon grass, garlic, spring onions, ginger, coriander roots, sugar, coconut milk, fish sauce and soy sauce into a food processor and process to a smooth purée. Pour the spice mixture over the chicken, turning until the chicken is thoroughly coated. Cover the dish with clingfilm and leave to marinate in the refrigerator for up to 8 hours.

Drain the chicken, reserving the marinade. Cook the chicken on the griddle over a medium–high heat, turning and brushing frequently with the reserved marinade, for 30–35 minutes, or until thoroughly cooked. Serve immediately, garnished with lime wedges.

4 chicken quarters or 8 chicken pieces

2 lemon grass stalks, roughly chopped

6 garlic cloves, roughly chopped

1 bunch spring onions, roughly chopped

2.5-cm/1-inch piece fresh root ginger, roughly chopped

1/2 bunch coriander roots, roughly chopped

1 tbsp palm sugar

125 ml/4 fl oz coconut milk

2 tbsp Thai fish sauce (nam pla)

2 tbsp dark soy sauce

lime wedges, to garnish

cook's tip

Palm sugar, coriander roots, coconut milk
and Thai fish sauce are all available from
specialist Chinese food shops. If you cannot
find palm sugar, then use brown sugar instead.

variation

Substitute the orange and yellow peppers
for red and green ones. Alternatively, just
use red peppers.

spicy chicken wings

Coated in a spicy marinade and served with a colourful pepper sauce, these delicious chicken wings are perfect as part of a summer lunch party. *SERVES 4*

Place the chicken wings in a large, shallow, non-metallic dish. Put the oil, soy sauce, ginger, garlic, lemon rind and juice, cinnamon, turmeric and honey into a food processor and process to a smooth purée. Season to taste with salt and pepper. Spoon the mixture over the chicken wings and turn until thoroughly coated, cover with clingfilm and leave to marinate in the refrigerator for up to 8 hours.

To make the sauce, brush the peppers with the oil and cook on the griddle, turning frequently, for 10 minutes, or until the skin is blackened and charred. Remove from the griddle and leave to cool slightly, then peel off the skins and discard the seeds. Put the flesh into a food processor with the yogurt and process to a smooth purée. Transfer to a bowl and stir in the soy sauce and chopped coriander.

Drain the chicken wings, reserving the marinade. Cook the wings on the griddle over a medium–high heat, turning and brushing the chicken frequently with the reserved marinade, for 8–10 minutes, or until thoroughly cooked. Serve immediately with the sauce.

16 chicken wings

4 tbsp sunflower oil

4 tbsp light soy sauce

5-cm/2-inch piece fresh root ginger, roughly chopped

2 garlic cloves, roughly chopped

juice and grated rind of 1 lemon

2 tsp ground cinnamon

2 tsp ground turmeric

4 tbsp clear honey

salt and pepper

sauce

2 orange peppers

2 yellow peppers

sunflower oil, for brushing

125 ml/4 fl oz natural yogurt

2 tbsp dark soy sauce

2 tbsp chopped fresh coriander

hot red chicken

In this adaptation of a traditional Indian recipe for Spring Chicken, chicken pieces are used, but you could substitute spatchcocked poussins if you prefer.

SERVES 4

1 tbsp curry paste

1 tbsp tomato ketchup

1 tsp Indian five-spice powder

1 fresh red chilli, deseeded and finely chopped

1 tsp Worcestershire sauce

1 tsp sugar

salt

8 skinless chicken pieces

vegetable oil, for brushing

naan bread, to serve

garnish

lemon wedges

fresh coriander sprigs

Place the curry paste, tomato ketchup, five-spice powder, chilli, Worcestershire sauce and sugar in a small bowl, and stir until the sugar has dissolved. Season to taste with salt.

Place the chicken pieces in a large, shallow, non-metallic dish and spoon the spice paste over them, rubbing it in well. Cover with clingfilm and leave to marinate in the refrigerator for up to 8 hours.

Remove the chicken from the spice paste, discarding any remaining paste, and then brush with oil. Cook the chicken on the griddle over a medium–high heat, turning occasionally, for 25–30 minutes. Briefly heat the naan bread on the griddle and serve with the chicken, garnished with lemon wedges and coriander sprigs.

variation
You can also serve this dish with garlic
naan bread or plenty of crusty bread, or
even freshly cooked rice.

chicken with saffron mash

The addition of fresh thyme, coriander and lemon juice complements the griddled chicken and saffron mash to perfection. Serve with freshly cooked steamed vegetables, such as carrots, broccoli and French beans, if you like. *SERVES 4*

550 g/1 lb 4 oz floury potatoes,
cut into chunks

1 garlic clove, peeled

1 tsp saffron threads, crushed

1.2 litres/2 pints chicken or vegetable stock

4 skinless, boneless chicken breasts,
trimmed of all visible fat

2 tbsp olive oil

1 tbsp lemon juice

1 tbsp chopped fresh thyme

1 tbsp chopped fresh coriander

1 tbsp coriander seeds, crushed

100 ml/3¹/₂ fl oz hot skimmed milk

salt and pepper

fresh thyme sprigs, to garnish

Put the potatoes, garlic and saffron in a large heavy-based saucepan, then add the stock and bring to the boil. Cover and simmer for 20 minutes, or until tender.

Meanwhile, brush the chicken breasts all over with half the olive oil and all of the lemon juice. Sprinkle with the fresh thyme and coriander and crushed coriander seeds. Heat a griddle pan, add the chicken and cook over a medium–high heat for 5 minutes on each side, or until the juices run clear when the meat is pierced with a skewer or the point of a knife. Alternatively, cook the chicken breasts under a preheated grill for 5 minutes on each side.

Drain the potatoes and return the contents of the sieve to the saucepan. Add the remaining olive oil and the milk, season to taste with salt and pepper and mash until smooth. Divide the saffron mash between 4 large, warmed serving plates, top with a piece of chicken and garnish with a few sprigs of fresh thyme. Serve.

variation

Serve sweet potato cream instead. Bake
550 g/1 lb 4 oz sweet potatoes for 1 hour.
Scoop out the flesh and mash. Heat and stir
in a little butter.

baked potatoes
with pesto chicken

Filled baked potatoes make wonderful comfort food on a cold day, but resist
the urge to add butter, soured cream or grated cheese. This potato needs only a green
salad to make a delicious light meal. *SERVES 4*

4 large potatoes
sunflower oil, for brushing
2 skinless, boneless chicken breasts,
about 115 g/4 oz each
250 ml/9 fl oz natural yogurt
1 tbsp pesto
green salad, to serve

Preheat the oven to 200°C/400°F/Gas Mark 6. Prick the potatoes all over with a fork and bake in the preheated oven for 1–1¹/₄ hours, or until soft and cooked through.

About 15 minutes before the potatoes are ready, heat a griddle pan and brush with a little sunflower oil. Add the chicken and cook over a medium–high heat for 5 minutes on each side, or until cooked through and tender. Meanwhile, put the yogurt and pesto in a bowl and mix until blended.

Slice the potatoes down the centre, almost right through, and open out. Cut the cooked chicken into slices. Divide the slices between the potatoes and top with the yogurt. Transfer to 4 warmed serving plates and serve with a green salad.

jamaican kebabs

What could be better on a hot summer's day than chicken kebabs flavoured with tropical fruit and a dash of rum? Serve with a crisp green salad for a filling lunch.

SERVES 4

2 mangoes

4 skinless, boneless chicken breasts, about 175 g/6 oz each, cut into 2.5-cm/1-inch cubes

finely grated rind and juice of 1 lime

1 tbsp dark rum

1 tbsp muscovado sugar

1 tsp ground mixed spice

Cut the mango into cubes. Using a sharp knife, cut the flesh from either side of the stone in 2 slices and trim off any flesh still clinging to it. Cut through the flesh in a diamond pattern, but do not cut through the skin. Turn the skin inside out and cut away the cubed flesh. Reserve until required. Place the chicken in a shallow, non-metallic dish. Sprinkle the lime rind and juice over the chicken and add the rum, sugar and mixed spice. Toss the chicken pieces until well coated, cover with clingfilm and leave to marinate in the refrigerator for 1 hour.

Drain the chicken, reserving the marinade. Thread the chicken pieces and mango cubes alternately onto 8 presoaked wooden skewers.

Heat the griddle and cook the chicken over a medium–high heat, turning and brushing frequently with the marinade, for 6–10 minutes, or until thoroughly cooked. Transfer the chicken to a large serving plate and serve immediately.

variation

Try substituting diced turkey breast for
the chicken, white wine for the rum and
cinnamon for the mixed spice.

cook's tip

Make sure that you buy genuine French
tarragon, as Russian tarragon is coarse and
can taste unpleasant. It is not worth using
dried tarragon, which has an insipid flavour.

tarragon turkey

This economical dish is quick and simple to prepare, and yet it tastes absolutely
wonderful, not least because poultry and tarragon have a natural affinity.

SERVES 4

4 turkey breasts, about 175 g/6 oz each
salt and pepper
4 tsp wholegrain mustard
8 fresh tarragon sprigs,
plus extra to garnish
4 smoked back bacon rashers
salad leaves, to serve

Season the turkey to taste with salt and pepper
and, using a round-bladed knife, spread the
mustard evenly over the turkey.

Place 2 tarragon sprigs on top of each turkey
breast and wrap a bacon rasher around it to hold
the herbs in place. Secure with a cocktail stick.

Heat the griddle and cook the turkey over a
medium–high heat for 5–8 minutes on each side.
Transfer to serving plates and garnish with
tarragon sprigs. Serve with salad leaves.

variation

To make a lemon sauce, simply substitute lemon juice for the orange juice, lemon slices for the orange slices and lemon balm for the chervil.

turkey breasts
with orange sauce

This is a fragrant, summery dish that needs nothing more than a crisp salad
and fresh rolls to make a satisfying supper. *SERVES 4*

4 turkey breast steaks, about 140 g/5 oz each	3–4 tbsp orange juice
salt and pepper	1 tbsp chopped fresh chervil
55 g/2 oz butter	*to garnish*
2 tbsp olive oil	orange slices
6 tbsp chicken stock	fresh chervil sprigs

Place each turkey breast steak in turn between 2 sheets of clingfilm and beat with the side of a rolling pin or the flat surface of a meat mallet until about 5 mm/¹/₄ inch thick. Season to taste with salt and pepper.

Melt half the butter with the oil in a large griddle pan. Add half the turkey steaks and cook over a high heat, turning once, for 3–4 minutes, or until lightly browned on both sides. Remove from the griddle pan, add the remaining turkey steaks, 1 at a time, and cook in the same way. Keep warm.

Pour the chicken stock into the griddle and bring to the boil, stirring and scraping up any sediment from the base of the pan. Add 3 tablespoons of the orange juice, the remaining butter and the chervil, and then reduce the heat to a simmer.

Return all the turkey steaks, with any meat juices, to the griddle. Simmer gently for 1 minute on each side. Taste and adjust the seasoning, adding more orange juice if necessary. Serve immediately, garnished with orange slices and chervil sprigs.

turkey with sun-dried tomato tapenade

Sun-dried tomatoes have a marvellously rich, fruity flavour that perfectly complements the marinated turkey – making this dish ideal for a hot summer's day. *SERVES 4*

4 turkey steaks

marinade
150 ml/5 fl oz white wine
1 tbsp white wine vinegar
1 tbsp olive oil
1 garlic clove, crushed
1 tbsp chopped fresh parsley
pepper

tapenade
225 g/8 oz sun-dried tomatoes in oil, drained
4 canned anchovy fillets, drained
1 garlic clove, crushed
1 tablespoon lemon juice
3 tablespoons chopped fresh parsley

Place the turkey steaks in a shallow, non-metallic dish. Mix all the marinade ingredients together in a jug, whisking well to mix. Pour the marinade over the turkey steaks, turning to coat. Cover with clingfilm and leave to marinate in the refrigerator for at least 1 hour.

To make the tapenade, put all the ingredients into a food processor and process to a smooth paste. Transfer to a bowl, cover with clingfilm and leave to chill in the refrigerator until required.

Drain the turkey steaks, reserving the marinade. Then heat the griddle and cook over a medium–high heat for 10–15 minutes, turning and brushing frequently with the reserved marinade. Transfer the turkey steaks to 4 large serving plates and top with the sun-dried tomato tapenade. Serve immediately.

variation

This dish would also work well with skinless, boneless chicken breasts. Make sure that the chicken is thoroughly cooked before serving.

variation

Substitute 4 pork chops for the duck and cook on a griddle over a medium-high heat for 8–9 minutes on each side.

fruity duck

Apricots and onions counteract the richness of the duck. Its high fat content makes it virtually self-basting, so it stays superbly moist. The duck looks particularly elegant garnished with spring onion tassels. *SERVES 4*

Using a sharp knife, cut a long slit in the fleshy side of each duck breast to make a pocket. Divide the apricots and shallots between the pockets and secure with skewers.

Mix the honey and sesame oil together in a small bowl and brush all over the duck. Sprinkle with the Chinese five-spice powder. To make the garnish, make a few cuts lengthways down the stem of each spring onion. Place in a bowl of ice-cold water and leave until the tassels open out. Drain well before using.

Heat the griddle and cook the duck over a medium–high flame for 6–8 minutes on each side. Remove the skewers, transfer to a large serving plate and garnish with the spring onion tassels. Serve immediately.

4 duck breasts

115 g/4 oz ready-to-eat dried apricots

2 shallots, thinly sliced

2 tbsp clear honey

1 tsp sesame oil

2 tsp Chinese five-spice powder

4 spring onions, to garnish

fish & seafood

THE full flavour and texture of fish and seafood are really brought out through griddling. In this section you can choose from a huge selection of recipes that include tuna, swordfish, salmon, sardines and tiger prawns.

mexican tuna

This spicy, Mexican-style tuna is sure to be a favourite with your adult guests.
The mouthwatering, hot flavours of cayenne, chilli and paprika are given
an added twist with a dash of tequila. *SERVES 4*

4 tuna steaks, about 175 g/6 oz each

fresh coriander sprigs, to garnish

lime wedges, to serve

sauce

2 tbsp sunflower oil

2 shallots, finely chopped

1 garlic clove, finely chopped

1 red pepper, deseeded and chopped

2 beef tomatoes, chopped

3 tbsp tomato ketchup

2 tbsp mild mustard

2 tbsp muscovado sugar

1 tbsp clear Mexican honey

1 tbsp cayenne pepper

1 tbsp chilli powder

1 tbsp paprika

1 tbsp tequila

To make the sauce, heat the oil in a heavy-based saucepan. Add the shallots and garlic, and cook over a low heat, stirring occasionally, for 5 minutes, or until softened but not coloured. Add the red pepper and cook for 1 minute, then add the tomatoes and simmer, stirring occasionally, for 20 minutes. Stir in the tomato ketchup, mustard, sugar, honey, cayenne, chilli powder, paprika and tequila and simmer for 20 minutes. Remove the saucepan from the heat and leave to cool.

Spoon the sauce into a food processor and process to a smooth purée. Rinse the fish under cold running water and pat dry with kitchen paper. Brush both sides of the tuna fillets with the sauce, place in a shallow dish, cover with clingfilm and leave to marinate in the refrigerator for 1 hour. Reserve the remaining sauce.

Brush the tuna steaks with the sauce and cook on a griddle over a medium–high heat, brushing frequently with the sauce, for 3 minutes on each side. Transfer to serving plates, garnish with fresh coriander sprigs and serve immediately with lime wedges.

variation

This recipe also works well with other oily fish, such as sea trout or salmon. Replace the lime wedges with lemon, if you prefer.

cajun spiced fish

Descended from immigrant French cuisine, Cajun cooking is marked by
a practical approach that makes the most of the ingredients available locally
from the countryside around New Orleans. *SERVES 4*

1 tbsp lime juice	*spice mix*
2 tbsp low-fat natural yogurt	1 tsp paprika
4 swordfish steaks,	1 tsp cayenne pepper
about 175 g/6 oz each	1 tsp ground cumin
sunflower oil, for brushing	1 tsp mustard powder
lemon wedges, to serve	1 tsp dried oregano

First make the spice mix by blending all the ingredients in a bowl. Mix the lime juice and yogurt in a separate bowl.

Pat the fish steaks dry with kitchen paper, then brush both sides with the yogurt mixture. Use your hands to coat both sides of the fish with the spice mix, rubbing it well into the flesh.

Brush a griddle with a little sunflower oil. Add the fish steaks and cook for 5 minutes over a medium–high heat, then turn over and cook for a further 4 minutes, or until the flesh flakes easily when tested with a fork. Serve straight from the pan with lemon wedges.

salmon teriyaki

This sweet but piquant Japanese-style teriyaki sauce complements
the richness of salmon superbly. Choose some really crisp salad leaves,
such as cos or iceberg, to serve with the warm sauce. *SERVES 4*

4 salmon fillets, about 175 g/6 oz each

sauce
1 tbsp cornflour
125 ml/4 fl oz dark soy sauce
4 tbsp mirin or medium-dry sherry
2 tbsp rice or cider vinegar
2 tbsp clear honey

to serve
1/2 cucumber
mixed salad leaves, torn into pieces
4 spring onions, thinly sliced diagonally

Rinse the salmon fillets under cold running
water, pat dry with kitchen paper and place in a
large, shallow, non-metallic dish. To make the
sauce, mix the cornflour and soy sauce together
in a jug until a smooth paste forms, then stir in the
remaining ingredients. Pour three-quarters of the
sauce over the salmon, turning to coat. Cover with
clingfilm and leave to marinate in the refrigerator
for 2 hours.

Cut the cucumber into batons, then arrange
the salad leaves, cucumber and spring onions on
4 serving plates. Pour the remaining sauce into
a saucepan and place on the griddle to
warm through.

Remove the salmon fillets from the dish
and reserve the marinade. Cook the salmon on the
griddle over a medium–high heat, brushing
frequently with the reserved marinade, for
3–4 minutes on each side. Transfer the salmon
fillets to the prepared serving plates and pour the
warmed sauce over them. Serve immediately.

variation

Replace the salmon with 4 x 115 g/4 oz chicken breast portions. Cut slashes in the meat before marinating and cook for about 15 minutes.

variation

If you like, substitute the chopped fresh parsley with the same amount of chopped fresh dill or thyme.

stuffed sardines

Fresh sardines are always a popular choice.
They are usually just plainly grilled, but here they are stuffed with herbs
and coated in a mild spice mixture. *SERVES 6*

15 g/¹/₂ oz fresh parsley, finely chopped

4 garlic cloves, finely chopped

12 fresh sardines, cleaned and scaled

3 tbsp lemon juice

85 g/3 oz plain flour

1 tsp ground cumin

salt and pepper

olive oil, for brushing

Place the parsley and garlic in a bowl and mix together. Rinse the fish inside and out under cold running water and pat dry with kitchen paper. Spoon the herb mixture into the fish cavities and pat the remainder all over the outside of the fish. Sprinkle the sardines with lemon juice and transfer to a large, shallow, non-metallic dish. Cover with clingfilm and leave to marinate in the refrigerator for 1 hour.

Mix the flour and ground cumin together in a bowl, then season to taste with salt and pepper. Spread out the seasoned flour on a large plate and gently roll the sardines in the flour to coat.

Brush the sardines with olive oil and cook on the griddle over a medium–high heat for 3–4 minutes on each side. Serve immediately.

mixed seafood brochettes

Seafood brochettes always look attractive and are perennially popular.
Here they are served with a flavoursome sauce for dipping. *SERVES 6*

2 tbsp sesame seeds

**500 g/1 lb 2 oz swordfish steaks
or monkfish fillet**

350 ml/12 fl oz dry white wine

2 tbsp sunflower oil

grated rind and juice of 2 limes

2 garlic cloves, finely chopped

salt and pepper

1¹/₂ tsp cornflour

2 tbsp water

2 tbsp chopped fresh coriander

12 prepared scallops

12 raw tiger prawns

Dry-fry the sesame seeds in a covered heavy-based frying pan until they begin to pop and give off their aroma. Remove from the heat and reserve. Cut the fish into 2.5-cm/1-inch cubes, then place in a shallow, non-metallic dish. Mix 200 ml/7 fl oz of the wine, the oil, lime rind and juice and garlic together in a jug and season to taste with salt and pepper. Pour half of this over the fish, turning to coat, and pour the remainder into a small saucepan. Cover the fish with clingfilm and leave to marinate in a cool place or the refrigerator for up to 1 hour.

Set the saucepan over a low heat and add the remaining wine. Mix the cornflour and water into a smooth paste and stir it into the saucepan, then bring to the boil, stirring constantly, and simmer until thickened. Remove the saucepan from the heat and stir in the coriander and roasted sesame seeds. Cover with a lid to keep warm.

Remove the fish from the marinade and thread onto 6 metal skewers, alternating with the scallops and prawns. Cook the brochettes on the griddle over a medium–high heat turning occasionally, for 5–8 minutes, or until the fish is cooked and the prawns have changed colour. Finally, when the brochettes are cooked, transfer them to a large serving plate and serve immediately with the sauce.

variation

For a budget dish, replace half the prawns
with tomato wedges and half the scallops
with onion wedges. Brush with the marinade
during cooking.

cook's tip

Coconut milk is not the same as the liquid from inside the fresh nut. It is available in cans from supermarkets and Chinese food shops.

coconut prawns

This classic Thai combination of flavours is perfect with prawns,
but would also go well with other fish and seafood. *SERVES 4*

Finely chop the spring onions and place in a large, shallow, non-metallic dish with the coconut milk, lime rind and juice, coriander and oil. Mix well and season to taste with pepper. Add the prawns, turning to coat. Cover with clingfilm and leave to marinate in the refrigerator for 1 hour.

Drain the prawns, reserving the marinade. Thread the prawns onto 8 long metal skewers.

Cook the skewers on a griddle over a medium–high heat, brushing with the reserved marinade and turning frequently, for 8 minutes, or until they have changed colour. Cook the lemon wedges, skin-side down on the griddle, for the last 5 minutes. Serve the prawns immediately, garnished with the hot lemon wedges and coriander sprigs.

6 spring onions

400 ml/14 fl oz coconut milk

finely grated rind and juice of 1 lime

4 tbsp chopped fresh coriander

2 tbsp sunflower oil

pepper

650 g/1 lb 7 oz raw tiger prawns

garnish

lemon wedges

fresh coriander sprigs

vegetables

GRIDDLED vegetables make ideal starters and are also excellent accompaniments to meat or fish. The six recipes included in this section are delicious and varied, from a Vegetable Platter dish to interesting kebab recipes.

prune, apricot & onion skewers

These flavoursome, fruity skewers would go well with plainly
grilled pork chops, duck breasts, lamb steaks or kebabs, as they
will counteract the richness of the meat. *SERVES 4*

500 g/1 lb 2 oz baby onions
175 g/6 oz prunes, stoned
225 g/8 oz dried apricots, stoned
5-cm/2-inch cinnamon stick
225 ml/8 fl oz white wine
2 tbsp chilli sauce
2 tbsp sunflower oil

Cut the tops off the onions and peel off the skin.
Reserve until required. Place the prunes, apricots,
cinnamon and wine in a heavy-based saucepan
and bring to the boil. Reduce the heat and simmer
for 5 minutes. Drain, reserving the cooking liquid,
and leave the fruit until cool enough to handle.

Return the cooking liquid and cinnamon stick
to the saucepan, return to the boil and boil until
reduced by half. Remove the saucepan from the
heat and remove and discard the cinnamon stick.
Stir in the chilli sauce and oil.

Thread the prunes, apricots and onions on to
several metal skewers. Cook on the griddle over
a medium–high heat, turning and brushing
frequently with the wine mixture, for 10 minutes.
Serve immediately.

cook's tip

Baby onions are also known as pearl onions
and have a delicate sweet flavour. If you
cannot find them, then use shallots or
1 white onion, cut into chunks.

cook's tip

When marinating vegetables, it is not
necessary to keep them in the refrigerator.
You can leave them in a cool place, covered
with clingfilm.

variation

If you prefer, replace the lemon mayonnaise
with plain mayonnaise, or try Creamy Pesto
(see page 79) instead.

vegetable platter

This cornucopia of griddled vegetables makes a wonderful vegetarian dish.
Equally, the vegetables can be served as accompaniments to meat or fish.

SERVES 4

2 red onions	2 tbsp chopped fresh marjoram
2 white onions	salt and pepper
2 fennel bulbs	1 green pepper
6 baby corn cobs	1 yellow pepper
12 cherry tomatoes	1 orange pepper
4 tbsp olive oil	1 red pepper
1 tbsp lemon juice	1 tbsp sunflower oil
3 garlic cloves, finely chopped	lemon mayonnaise, to serve

Using a sharp knife, cut the red and white onions in half and reserve until required. Blanch the fennel and corn cobs in a large saucepan of boiling water for 2 minutes. Drain, refresh under cold running water and drain again. Cut the fennel bulbs in half and place in a large, shallow, non-metallic dish. Cut the corn cobs in half across the centre and add to the dish with the tomatoes and onions.

Mix the oil, lemon juice, garlic and marjoram in a jug and season to taste with salt and pepper. Pour the mixture over the vegetables, cover with clingfilm and leave to marinate for 1 hour.

Drain the vegetables, reserving the marinade. Thread the corn and cherry tomatoes alternately on to presoaked wooden skewers. Brush the peppers with oil and cook on the griddle over a medium–high heat, turning frequently, for 10 minutes. Add the onion and fennel to the griddle and cook, brushing with the marinade, for 5 minutes. Turn the onion and fennel and brush with marinade. Add the skewers, brush with marinade and cook, turning and brushing frequently with more marinade, for 10 minutes. Transfer the vegetables to a large plate and serve with the lemon mayonnaise.

aubergines with tsatziki

This makes a delicious starter for a party or can be served as part
of a selection of vegetarian meze. *SERVES 4*

2 tbsp olive oil

salt and pepper

2 aubergines, thinly sliced

tsatziki

¹/₂ cucumber

200 ml/7 fl oz natural Greek yogurt

4 spring onions, finely chopped

1 garlic clove, finely chopped

3 tbsp chopped fresh mint

salt and pepper

1 fresh mint sprig, to garnish

To make the tsatziki, finely chop the cucumber. Place the yogurt in a bowl and beat well until smooth. Stir in the cucumber, spring onions, garlic and mint. Season to taste with salt and pepper. Transfer to a serving bowl, cover with clingfilm and leave everything to chill in the refrigerator until required.

Season the olive oil with salt and pepper, then brush the aubergine slices with the oil.

Cook the aubergines on the griddle over a high heat for 5 minutes on each side, brushing with more oil, if necessary. Transfer to a large serving plate and serve immediately with the tsatziki, garnished with a mint sprig.

cook's tip

An alternative dip to serve with the aubergines can be made by blending 300 ml/ 10 fl oz soured cream with 2 crushed garlic cloves. Season and chill before serving.

variation

If you prefer, replace the green pepper with a sweeter orange or red pepper and the aubergine with 1 courgette, cut into chunks.

cook's tip

Christophene, also known as chayote, is a pear-shaped gourd widely used in Caribbean cooking. If you cannot find it, use pumpkin or courgettes instead.

spicy caribbean kebabs

Bring a taste of the tropics to your parties with these sizzling vegetable kebabs.
They make a delicious vegetarian main course and are also suitable for vegans. *SERVES 4*

1 corn cob

1 christophene, peeled and
cut into chunks

1 ripe plantain, peeled and cut
into thick slices

1 aubergine, cut into chunks

1 red pepper, deseeded and cut
into chunks

1 green pepper, deseeded and cut
into chunks

1 onion, cut into wedges

8 button mushrooms

4 cherry tomatoes

marinade

150 ml/5 fl oz tomato juice

4 tbsp sunflower oil

4 tbsp lime juice

3 tbsp dark soy sauce

1 shallot, finely chopped

2 garlic cloves, finely chopped

1 fresh green chilli, deseeded and
finely chopped

1/2 tsp ground cinnamon

pepper

Using a sharp knife, remove the husks and silks from the corn cob and cut into 2.5-cm/1-inch thick slices. Blanch the christophene chunks in boiling water for 2 minutes. Drain, refresh under cold running water and drain again. Place the christophene chunks in a large bowl with the corn cob slices and the remaining ingredients.

Mix all the marinade ingredients together in a jug, seasoning to taste with pepper. Pour the marinade over the vegetables, tossing to coat. Cover with clingfilm and leave to marinate in the refrigerator for 3 hours.

Drain the vegetables, reserving the marinade. Thread the vegetables onto several metal skewers. Cook on the griddle over a high heat, turning and brushing frequently with the reserved marinade, for 10–15 minutes. Transfer to a large serving plate and serve immediately.

cheese & red onion kebabs

Red onions have a mild, sweet flavour and retain their attractive colour when cooked. Here, they are griddled with apples and salty cheese for a wonderful combination of flavours and textures. *SERVES 4*

3 red onions
450 g/1 lb halloumi cheese, cut into
2.5-cm/1-inch cubes
2 tart eating apples, cored and
cut into wedges
4 tbsp olive oil
1 tbsp cider vinegar
1 tbsp Dijon mustard
1 garlic clove, finely chopped
1 tsp finely chopped sage
salt and pepper

Cut the onions into wedges, then place in a large, shallow, non-metallic dish with the cheese and apples. Mix the oil, vinegar, mustard, garlic and sage together in a jug and season to taste with salt and pepper.

Pour the marinade over the onions, cheese and apples, tossing to coat. Cover with clingfilm and leave to marinate in the refrigerator for 2 hours.

Drain the onions, cheese and apples, reserving the marinade. Thread the onions, cheese and apples alternately onto several metal skewers. Cook on the griddle over a high heat, turning and brushing frequently with the reserved marinade, for 10–15 minutes. Transfer to a large serving plate and serve immediately.

variation

If baby vegetables are not available, you can cut 2 aubergines into slices and cut 2 courgettes in half lengthways instead.

cook's tip

This home-made pesto mixture, without the added yogurt, will keep in a screw-top jar in the refrigerator for up to 3 days. Pour a layer of olive oil over the top to stop it drying out.

griddled vegetables with creamy pesto

Vegetables, especially baby varieties, taste wonderful when cooked on the griddle. Here they are served with a delicious pesto, which complements them perfectly. Serve with griddled meat. *SERVES 4*

To make the creamy pesto, place the basil, pine kernels, garlic and sea salt in a mortar and pound to a paste with a pestle. Gradually work in the Parmesan cheese, then gradually stir in the oil. Place the yogurt in a small serving bowl and stir in 3–4 tablespoons of the pesto mixture. Cover with clingfilm and leave to chill in the refrigerator until required. Store any leftover pesto mixture in a screw-top jar in the refrigerator.

Prepare the vegetables. Cut the onion and fennel bulb into wedges, trim the aubergines and courgettes, deseed and halve the peppers and cut the tomatoes in half. Brush the vegetables with oil and season to taste with salt and pepper.

Cook the aubergines and peppers on the griddle for 3 minutes, then add the courgettes, onion and tomatoes and cook, turning occasionally and brushing with more oil if necessary, for a further 5 minutes. Transfer to a large serving plate and serve immediately with the pesto, garnished with a basil sprig.

1 red onion

1 fennel bulb

4 baby aubergines

4 baby courgettes

1 orange pepper

1 red pepper

2 beef tomatoes

2 tbsp olive oil

salt and pepper

creamy pesto

55 g/2 oz fresh basil leaves

15 g/1/2 oz pine kernels

1 garlic clove

pinch of coarse sea salt

25 g/1 oz freshly grated Parmesan cheese

50 ml/2 fl oz extra virgin olive oil

150 ml/5 fl oz natural Greek yogurt

1 fresh basil sprig, to garnish

desserts

HERE are six really fabulous and truly mouth-watering griddled fruit recipes that show off the art of griddling to the full. Hot griddled fruit is both juicy and crunchy and is delicious served with a contrasting accompaniment such as ice cream or mascarpone.

PART FIVE

special peach melba

The elegant simplicity of this rich, fruity dessert makes it the perfect end to a special occasion party. *SERVES 4*

2 large peaches, peeled, halved and stoned
1 tbsp light brown sugar
1 tbsp Amaretto liqueur
450 g/1 lb fresh raspberries, plus extra to decorate
115 g/4 oz icing sugar
600 ml/1 pint vanilla ice cream

Place the peach halves in a large, shallow dish and sprinkle with the brown sugar. Pour the Amaretto liqueur over them, cover with clingfilm and leave to marinate for 1 hour.

Meanwhile, using the back of a spoon, press the raspberries through a fine sieve set over a bowl. Discard the contents of the sieve. Stir the icing sugar into the raspberry purée. Cover the bowl with clingfilm and leave to chill in the refrigerator until required.

Drain the peach halves, reserving the marinade. Cook on the griddle, turning and brushing frequently with the reserved marinade, for 3–5 minutes. To serve, put 2 scoops of vanilla ice cream in each of 4 sundae glasses, top with a peach half and spoon the raspberry sauce over it. Decorate with whole raspberries and serve.

cook's tip

For the best results, remove the vanilla ice
cream from the freezer 20 minutes before
serving and leave in the refrigerator.

If you prefer, you can cut the pineapple into
cubes or quarters and thread onto skewers before
brushing with the rum mixture and cooking.

totally tropical pineapple

The delicious aroma of fresh pineapple and rum as this succulent, mouthwatering dessert is cooking will transport you to a Caribbean beach. The ground ginger adds just a touch of spice. *SERVES 4*

Using a sharp knife, cut off the crown of the pineapple, then cut the fruit into 2-cm/3/4-inch thick slices. Cut away the peel from each slice and flick out the 'eyes' with the point of the knife. Stamp out the cores with an apple corer or small pastry cutter.

Mix the rum, sugar, ginger and butter together in a jug, stirring constantly, until the sugar has dissolved. Brush the pineapple rings with the rum mixture.

Cook the pineapple rings on the griddle for 3–4 minutes on each side. Transfer to serving plates and serve immediately with the remaining rum mixture poured over them.

1 pineapple

3 tbsp dark rum

2 tbsp muscovado sugar

1 tsp ground ginger

4 tbsp unsalted butter, melted

peaches with
creamy mascarpone filling

If you prepare these in advance, all you have to do is pop the peaches
on the griddle when you are ready to serve them. They make a great
finale to any party. *SERVES 4*

4 peaches
175 g/6 oz mascarpone cheese
40 g/1¹/₂ oz pecan nuts or
walnuts, chopped
1 tsp sunflower oil
4 tbsp maple syrup

Cut the peaches in half and remove the stones. If you are preparing this recipe in advance, press the peach halves together and wrap in clingfilm until required.

Mix the mascarpone cheese and pecans together in a bowl until well combined. Leave to chill in the refrigerator until required.

Brush the peach halves with a little sunflower oil and place on the griddle over a medium–high heat. Cook the peach halves for 5–10 minutes, turning once, until hot.

Transfer the peach halves to a serving dish and top with the mascarpone and nut mixture. Drizzle the maple syrup over the peaches and mascarpone filling and serve immediately.

cook's tip

If you are following a low-fat diet, use low-fat thick natural yogurt or low-fat crème fraîche instead of the mascarpone cheese.

cook's tip

Always try to find the best-quality chocolate
that you can buy. Try to break the chocolate
into pieces of roughly the same size, so they
will all melt at the same rate.

cinnamon fruit
with chocolate sauce

Fresh fruit kebabs are coated with spicy butter before griddling and are then served with an easy-to-prepare, rich chocolate sauce. *SERVES 4*

4 slices fresh pineapple	*sauce*
2 kiwi fruit, peeled and quartered	225 g/8 oz plain chocolate
12 strawberries, hulled	25 g/1 oz unsalted butter
1 tbsp melted unsalted butter	125 g/4^1/$_2$ oz caster sugar
1 tsp ground cinnamon	125 ml/4 fl oz evaporated milk
1 tbsp orange juice	1 tsp vanilla essence
	4 tbsp Kahlúa

To make the sauce, break the chocolate into pieces and melt with the butter in a saucepan over a low heat. Stir in the sugar and evaporated milk and cook, stirring, until the sugar has dissolved and the sauce has thickened. Transfer to a heatproof bowl and keep hot.

Cut the pineapple slices into chunks. Thread the pineapple chunks, kiwi fruit and strawberries alternately onto several presoaked wooden skewers. Mix the butter, cinnamon and orange juice together in a small bowl. Brush the fruit kebabs all over with the cinnamon butter.

Cook the kebabs on the griddle, turning and brushing frequently with any remaining cinnamon butter, for 3–5 minutes, or until golden. Just before serving, stir the vanilla essence and Kahlúa into the sauce and drizzle over the kebabs.

banana sizzles

Bananas are particularly sweet and delicious when griddled –
and conveniently come with their own protective wrapping. *SERVES 4*

Beat the butter with the rum, orange juice, sugar and cinnamon in a small bowl until thoroughly blended and smooth.

Place all the bananas, without peeling, on a hot griddle and cook, turning frequently, for 6–8 minutes, or until the skins are blackened.

Transfer the bananas to serving plates, slit the skins and cut partially through the flesh lengthways. Divide the flavoured butter between the bananas, decorate with orange zest and serve.

3 tbsp butter, softened

2 tbsp dark rum

1 tbsp orange juice

4 tbsp muscovado sugar

pinch of ground cinnamon

4 bananas

orange zest, to decorate

cook's tip
Look for 'pure' or '100 per cent' maple syrup,
which is quite expensive. Cheaper varieties
may be blended with other types of syrup.

griddled fruit
with maple syrup

Slices of juicy fruit are coated in a rich maple syrup sauce as they
cook on the griddle. *SERVES 4*

1 mango, peeled and stoned

1 papaya

2 bananas

2 peaches, halved, stoned and peeled

1 ogen melon, halved and seeded

115 g/4 oz unsalted butter, diced

4 tbsp maple syrup

pinch of ground mixed spice

Thickly slice the mango and remove the stone, then peel off the skin and cut the flesh into slices. Using a sharp knife, cut the papaya in half and remove the seeds, then cut the halves into thick slices and peel off the skin. Peel the bananas and cut in half lengthways. Slice the peach halves. Cut the melon halves into thin wedges, then cut the flesh away from the rind.

Put the butter and maple syrup into a food processor and process until thoroughly blended and smooth. Pour the flavoured butter over the fruit and sprinkle with a little mixed spice.

Cook the fruit on the griddle over a medium–high heat, turning occasionally, for 10 minutes. Remove from the griddle and serve immediately.

variation

Sprinkle the fruit kebabs with chopped
walnuts or pecan nuts before serving,
if you wish.

toffee fruit kebabs

Serve these fruit kebabs with a sticky toffee sauce. They are perfect for serving at parties. *SERVES 4*

2 dessert apples, cored and cut into wedges

2 firm pears, cored and cut into wedges

juice of $^1/_2$ lemon

25 g/1 oz light muscovado sugar

$^1/_4$ tsp ground allspice

25 g/1 oz unsalted butter, melted

sauce

125 g/4$^1/_2$ oz butter

100 g/3$^1/_2$ oz light muscovado sugar

6 tbsp double cream

Toss the apples and pears in the lemon juice to prevent any discoloration.

Mix the sugar and allspice together and sprinkle over the fruit. Thread the fruit pieces onto skewers.

To make the toffee sauce, place the butter and sugar in a saucepan and heat, stirring gently, until the butter has melted and the sugar has dissolved. Add the cream to the saucepan and bring to the boil. Boil for 1–2 minutes, then leave to cool slightly.

Meanwhile, place the fruit kebabs on a hot griddle and cook for 5 minutes, turning and basting frequently with the melted butter, until the fruit is just tender. Transfer the fruit kebabs to warmed serving plates and serve with the cooled toffee sauce.

index